Eugene Victor Debs

Lecture at the Fargo Opera House

Eugene Victor Debs

Lecture at the Fargo Opera House

ISBN/EAN: 9783744659109

Printed in Europe, USA, Canada, Australia, Japan

Cover: Foto ©ninafisch / pixelio.de

More available books at **www.hansebooks.com**

VERBATIM REPORT

OF THE

LECTURE

DELIVERED BY

EUGENE V. DEBS,

AT

Opera House, Fargo, N. D.

MARCH 6, 1895.

Issued by the T. L. P. U. No. 1, Fargo.

G. P. VAN KLEECK, Chairman.
E. G. ECKER, - Secretary.

Independent Pub. Co.-Fargo.

LECTURE

BY EUGENE V. DEBS.

LADIES AND GENTLEMEN: First of all permit me to thank the reverend gentleman who has just presented me, from the very depths of my heart for his beautiful words, which I appreciate far beyond the power of language to express.

There are many thousands of our people who view with apprehension and alarm the wide-spread unrest that pervades our social, industrial and political system, and taking counsel of their doubts and fears, they arrive at the conclusion that the prophecy of McCauley is about to be fulfilled, that "self-government is to be an administrative failure," and that the sun of our republic is to set in universal gloom.

I am not of that number. Having faith in the ever-increasing intelligence of the masses, I am persuaded that the grand old ship of state, with her precious cargo of human hopes and aspirations, will breast all of the billows and weather all of the storms, and finally safely reach her destined port.

I admit that the immediate outlook is not rich with promise, and yet there is a hopeful view to be taken of the situation. The feudal system gave way to the competitive system, which in my judgment is now in the throes of dissolution, and the competitive system has to give way and fall into the co-operative system. We have met to-night for the purpose of speaking of the more important phases of the late great strike, the greatest industrial upheaval of modern times.

If there are those present (as I do not doubt there are) who know me only as I have been described in the papers, and who are therefore prejudiced, I ask them in all fairness to dismiss that prejudice and give me the benefit of a fair and impartial hearing. In what I shall have to say to-night, it will be my purpose, as it has always been my purpose, to present the issues fairly, to see an injustice upon one side as quickly as upon another, and do equal and exact justice to both.

First of all, let it be understood that the Pullman company is capitalized at $31,000,000, according to their own statement. They have an undivided surplus of $25,000,000. The company of Pullman own the town of Pullman absolutely. There is not an inch of free soil there, nor is there a free man, woman or child; a species of serfdom that, if known, would horrify the world.

Preliminary to what I shall have to say, let me introduce the words of a clergyman, Rev. Carwardine, for two years a resident minister in Pullman, a gentleman of unimpeachable integrity, widely known and as widely respected. There is an introduction to his book by another minister of the gospel, who made a visit to Pullman, the Rev. Mr. Driver, and he says that this book is filled with facts, for which facts the author is not responsible. If sometimes the author's spirit flames with indignation, let it be remembered that it is against heartless tyranny and in defense of long silent and outraged innocence. The author means neither to minify nor magnify. He has not fallen into misrepresentation. The statements can all be verified again and again. In his work Mr. Carwardine says: "The great trouble with this Pullman system is that it is not what it pretends to be. It is a civilized relic of European serfdom."

We all enjoy living here because there is an equality of interest, and we have a common enemy, the Company, but our daily prayer is, "Lord, keep us from dying here." An eminent writer in Harper's Monthly in 1884, on Pullman, declared that at that time, ten years ago, its great faults were: "Bad administration in respect to the employment, retention and promotion of employees. Change is constant in men and officers and each new superior appears to have his own friends, whom he appoints to desirable positions. Favoritism and nepotism exist; natural dissatisfaction, a powerful prevalience of petty jealousies, discouragements of superior excellence, frequent change of residents, and an all-pervading feeling of insecurity."

The writer further declares that it is not an American idea. It is a species of benevolent feudalism, and as to its morals, the writer says: "The prevailing tendency at that day was the desire to beat the Company."

It is generally agreed that the maximum average wage paid at the time of the strike was $1.85. As to the lowest wages, it is difficult to average. The wages are paid every two weeks. Two checks are given to each employee—one a rent check, the other a pay check. Wages are paid at the bank. When they go to the bank they receive their two weeks' pay, the half month's rent is taken out, and the pay check cashed. The scenes enacted at the bank during last winter were pitiable. Not only was the current rent urgently demanded, but back rent was asked for under circumstances in many cases entirely uncalled for. After deducting rent the men invariably had only from one to six dollars or so, on which to live for two weeks. One man has a pay check in his possession of two cents after paying rent. He has never cashed it, preferring to keep it as a memento. He has it framed. Another I saw the other day for seven cents. It was dated September, 1893. The man had worked as a skilled mechanic for ten hours a day for twelve days and earned $9.07. He keeps a widowed mother, and pays the rent, the house being in his name. His half month's rent amounted to $9. The seven cents was his, but he has never claimed it. Another employee had 47 cents coming to him on his pay check, and then was asked if he would not apply that on his back rent. He was indignant. He replied: "If Mr. Pullman needs that 47 cents worse than I do, let him have it." He left it.

These instances might be indefinitely multiplied. Let me recite one that came under my personal observation. There was a young woman working there under the name of Jennie Curtis. Her father died last August a year ago indebted to the Company $65 for rent. The next day after the funeral the young woman was notified that if she expected to continue in the service of that Company she would be expected to sign an agreement to pay to the Company in installments the $65 owed by her father at the time of his death.

She told me that after making the payment of the regular installment, there was not enough left to supply herself and the little brother and sister with the necessaries of life, and she had to depend upon the charity of the neighbors. These instances might be multiplied indefinitely.

A child born at Pullman is born in a Pullman house, is rocked in a Pullman cradle, is educated in a Pullman school, attends a Pullman church, works, of course, in a Pullman shop, and when at last death (sometimes the poor man's best friend) has wrung from the unfortunate victim the last despairing sigh, he is wrapped in a Pullman shroud, placed in a Pullman casket, drawn in a Pullman hearse to a Pullman cemetery and buried in a Pullman grave. That is the story of a human life at Pullman. The wages are so adjusted to each other that in some way every dollar earned by the employees finds its way back into the coffers of the Pullman Company.

During the year preceding the strike, the wages were reduced three times, and under the last reduction there was not enough left to supply the necessaries of life. They were patient to a degree that defied exaggeration and I say here tonight that no man with a heart throbbing in his bosom could have gone to Pullman and made investigation without coming away in sympathy with the strikers.

While there were three reductions in the wages of these employees, there was no reduction in the rents. The testimony was given by a number of real estate experts that the rents at Pullman were from twenty-five to forty per cent higher than they were in any of the adjoining towns. The claim was made by the Company that they were obliged on account of the depression of the times to make some reduction. They did not make the reductions on account of the depression of the times, but they did make them to crush out their competitors, because they could have their work done for nothing. For the item of rent the employees were in debt to the Company at the time of the strike $70,000.

They were getting deeper and deeper into the debt of the Pullman Company every day, and they realized that it was only a question of time until they should be mortgaged body and soul and their children and their children's children to the Pullman corporation forever.

For taking part in this strike I have been condemned by a great many people and I have lost the respect of a great many others, but I have kept my own. I have been true to myself. Before I conclude my arguments, I know I shall be able to convince you that those men, in striking for their rights, did only as you would have done, had you been similarly oppressed.

The Pullman Company is one of the wealthiest on the continent. It increased its capital from 1883 to 1889, a period of six years, $12,000,000, or two million dollars a year. There never has been a reduction, even to the fraction of a per cent, in their dividend. Regularly they have declared their dividend, adding yearly to their capital. They had no excuse for grinding their old and trusted employees into the dust. They did it simply because they thought they had the power to do it, as remorseless as a conflagration. They did not hear the music of groans and sighs at Pullman.

The employees of the Pullman Company did not want to strike. Mr. Carver Dean said they did everything that honorable men could do to avoid a strike. At last they appointed a committee and called on the officials of the city of Chicago and Mr. Pullman happened to be there. Mr. Pullman, let me say, who poses before the world as a philanthropist, is the veriest hypocrite, and I propose to strip him of his mask and let you see him as he is. When his employees came to this meeting his conscience (if he had one) must have smitten him, and he thrust his hand into his pocket and he assumed the expression of a Pharisee as he said, "Have I not been a father to you?" When the committee told it to me I said, "The good Lord deliver me from that kind of a father. I had a good deal rather take my chances on being an orphan."

Then he said, "I will investigate your grievances," and then for the first time they saw a glimmer of hope. They said, "At least our grievances will be investigated by the officials and there is a bare possibility that justice may be done." And the very next morning the *committee were discharged.* That is the way in which the Pullman company kept faith with its employees; had promised to investigate and then discharged the committee.

That day every man, woman and child withdrew from the service of the company, and I honor them for it. I am not unmindful of the fact that a great many people are opposed to the strike. I confess that I am myself, but on account of the overmastering greed of some corporation, the time comes now and then when you have got to choose between a strike and degradation, and when that time comes, I believe in striking with all the force at my command, and then I feel as Jackson did about it, "By the eternal, I will take all the consequences of my acts." And when my case is called they will not have to issue a bench warrant. I will be there to toe the mark of duty. I will not take my private car and leave for the seashore, as did Pullman.

I would remind you here tonight that we live under a striking government; that there is not a star nor a stripe in the American flag that does not tell of a strike. At Lexington, where the shot was fired that was heard around the world, at Concord, and all along that track of gloom and glory, there was one continuous succession of strikes for liberty and independence, and had it not been for the magnificent courage and patriotism of the revolutionary fathers in striking for their rights, we would have been British subjects to-night instead of sovereign American citizens.

Every inch of progress that has been made in this world was made by virtue of a strike, and the revolutionary fathers were not only strikers, but they were a class of boycotters, and so were the revolutionary mothers as well. You have often heard the boycott spoken of as a crime. The revolutionary fathers put the boycott on tea, and they did not only boycott, but they destroyed property as well. They went down to Boston harbor and made a teapot of it, and the revolutionary mothers said "Amen, we will go without our tea."

There were tories who said Washington was a dangerous demagogue, but now the school children honor his memory. The difference between a demagogue and a demi-god is only about a quarter of a century. A good many people say, "We must maintain law and order." Well, suppose Washington and Jefferson and Franklin and Paine had been for law and order. They trampled the law under foot with impunity in as holy a cause as ever prompted men to action in this world.

I am for law and order myself, but I want it to be the right kind of law, and I want it enforced against all people alike. The trouble has been in this country that our judicial nets have been so adjusted as to catch the minnows and let the whales slip through. If the metropolitan press of this country had been published in the days of Washington, they would have denounced these grand patriots. They were denounced by the weak and by those who said "Why don't you let well enough alone? You will bring trouble upon the country if you continue in lawlessness and riot and bloodshed." And then those patriots expanded to the proportions of freemen, and said, "If there has got to be war in order to get independence, let it come now, that our children may enjoy the blessings of peace." There were those who thought an agitator was perfectly disreputable, but it was simply a question of agitation or stagnation.

I am an agitator. I do not blush when I admit it. I am going to do all that is in my power to change conditions. They do not suit me. I do not see how any man with a heart throbbing in him can be satisfied with the conditions as they are now in this country. There are those who say "Let well enough alone." If this is well enough, what could be bad enough? Progress is born of agitation. The men who agitate pay the penalties, and some of the penalties they pay are misrepresentations. They are misrepresented by those who cannot conceive of a pure, disinterested motive. The motives of the men who incur all these penalties and who invite social condemnation are as far above the motives of their detractors as the stars are above the rolling prairie.

I know there are those who believe with Walpole, that "Every man has his price." Walpole was a scoundrel and had his price, or he never would have conceived that infamy. But there are men in this world who have not got their price; there are men who are pure and incorruptible; there are men who cannot be influenced by all the wealth of the corporations, nor can they be silenced by all the penalties that may attach to them. Those men are the "salt of the earth," as Christ said, the light and the hope of this world. I have made up my mind long since that I am going to be true to myself.

Many people say that we ought to consult public opinion, do not do anything that shocks society. Let me say to you tonight in all candor, that I have not the slightest faith in public opinion as a guide. As a general proposition public opinion is wrong. I admit that it gets right in the course of 3,000 or 4,000 years, but that is too long for an ordinary mortal to wait. It was public opinion that kept up the infamous institution of slavery for years. It was public opinion that put Wendall Phillips (as noble a heart as ever beat "betwixt us and the mercy seat") in the pillory in his native town and spat upon him. It was public opinion that committed those monstrous outrages against Harriet Martineau, as noble a woman as ever breathed. She was to go to Ohio and make speeches against slavery and the people arose and said that if she put her foot on Ohio soil they would strangle the life out of her body.

It was public opinion that murdered John Brown, because he was tender and humane enough to say that property in man is a crime. Wendell Phillips was born with a silver spoon in his mouth. He belonged to the aristocratic classes. He could have been universally respected, he could have been a social lion, but he preferred to speak out against an institution that fired his noble soul with indignation. He ostracised himself. Society closed its doors in his face and poured its filth upon his head, but he stood erect; he had the courage of his convictions. However severe the alternative, he did not falter in his God-given mission, and he lived long enough to see the inhuman institution of slavery destroyed.

Had Phillips and Garrison and all the rest of their coadjutors been silent, had they believed in law and order, had they feared to incur the abuse that comes from agitating (especially when the old institution is the subject of attack) the institution of slavery would have been upon our soil yet, would pollute the free atmosphere of the republic.

It is precisely so with the working people of this country. Admitted or not, as you feel about it, but the fact is that the industrialists of this country are in serfdom; are in bondage from which there is no escape for the individual except possibly through the back door of suicide. Is the fact a haggard one? So much the worse for our much vaunted civilization. But I do not take a gloomy view of the future. . I believe with Fitch that the common people of this country are beginning to think for themselves.

In the past they have been satisfied to do their thinking by proxy, but they are now beginning to do something for themselves. The working people are the hope of the future. It is here, under the flag of the fourty-four stars, that workingmen are beginning to ask why it is that they must press their rags still closer lest they jostle against the silken garment which their fingers have made; why it is that they must walk weary and shelterless in the shadow of homes that they have erected, but may not enter.

Workingmen are beginning to think, and they will soon begin to act; they will not beg for their rights, but they will take them, not in lawlessness, not in pillage and riot, but in a lawful manner. They will take them by the power of the ballot, the weapon that "falls as lightly as the snowflake falls upon the sod, yet executes a free man's will as lightning does the will of God."

They are the cries of the people because of centuries of oppression and toil and martyrdom and they know that the people of a free country will hear that cry, because here labor is the king; the conservator of all capital. Labor makes the forest monarch fall low unto the earth and siezes the monster and transforms it; labor smites at the adamantine doors of vast treasure chambers, and shall not workingmen carry their own? Who shall doubt it? When the mariner passing over the tropic seas looks for relief, he turns his eyes to the southern cross, and as midnight approaches, the southern cross begins to bend and the stars begin to change their places, and the Almighty marks the passage of time on the heavens. Let labor everywhere take heart of hope, for the cross is bending, and the midnight is passing and "Joy cometh in the morning."

Here let me remind you (returning to the subject) that the Pullman employes never asked the Pullman Company to do anything but to submit their trouble to arbitration. I believe, as they believe, in the American principle of arbitration, and if a man will not submit to it, it is evidence that he has no faith in the justice of his cause.

The employees simply said, "Let us arbitrate," and the company said, "There is nothing to arbitrate," and Mr. Pullman (who has a happy faculty of getting away when he is wanted) went to the seashore until his old and trusted employees should be starved back into his employ on his terms. We made this proposition. We said, "Let the Pullman company select two representatives, let the judges of the Circuit court appoint two representatives, and let these four appoint a fifth. We will not ask for a representative on the board at all. Let that board of five decide if there is anything to arbitrate, and if that board decides that there is nothing to arbitrate, the employees will go back to work.

But the Company insisted that it did not have anything to arbitrate for two reasons: The first was that they knew that no five men could have been found in the City of Chicago who would not have decided in favor of the employees. There was another more important reason. They knew that if such an investigation would have been made, a state of affairs would have been disclosed that would have horrified the world. That was why they were opposed from first to last to the question as to whether there was anything to arbitrate.

The delegates of the A. R. U. met in convention on the 12th day of June, and many of the delegates visited Pullman in person. I went there myself. I could not believe the report of the horrible conditions at Pullman. I went there twice, from home to home, from hovel to hovel. I met the wives of some of the employees and the wives of some of them I did not meet, because they did not have clothes to make them presentable.

I saw children suffering hunger and in rags, the most pitiable spectacle I ever saw in my life, more rags than I have ever seen before, anyhow. The delegates visited there and their hearts were touched. It could not be otherwise, and they said, "We will make a final effort to adjust this trouble." They appointed a committee and asked the Pullman Company if they would not give their employees a hearing, and they dismissed them without consideration. They went a second time and were treated with disdain and contempt.

The mayor and city council of Chicago visited them, but all of their efforts were unavailing; the Pullman Company stood stubborn as adamant. Then the committee said, "If the Pullman Company refuses to show any disposition to adjust this difference with their employees, then we, as members of the American Railway Union, will not join in the wrong." So they decided by the vote of 425 delegates.

You hear that I am responsible for the strike. I did not even have a vote in ordering the strike, but 425 sturdy men, after having exhausted every effort that kindliness could suggest, voted without a dissenting voice to refuse to handle Pullman cars if the Pullman Company did not show some disposition to treat with its starving employees. I cordially endorsed the action of the delegates. They could not have done otherwise without having been cowards and apostates. The Pullman employees were members of their organization; they were their brothers and their sisters; they were the victims of conditions which they could not avoid or control.

It was the duty of their brothers to go to their rescue and they did it and I am proud of it, and when all the truth is known, they will not be obliged to blush for their conduct. But before I go into this part of the argument, I want to show you that there were other influences in operation that justified the action of these delegates. I hold in my hand a clipping from the Chicago Herald of May 5th, 1893, six weeks before the American Railway Union was instituted. The Chicago Herald cannot be charged with being unduly friendly with labor organizations. The three great papers of Chicago were against us and burdened the wire with falsehoods. The Chicago Herald says in regard to the Managers' Organization: "Setting forth the reasons as given by the General Managers' Association for forming an organization, principle of which, that in case of a strike on any one road which was a member of the association, caused by a reduction of wages, which was shortly to be put into effect one line at a time, the other roads would force their employees into a combination for the purpose of quelling the strike or else compelling them all to go out on a sympathetic strike for mutual protection."

If a sympathy strike is a crime and conspiracy, as has been held, and if the Managers' Association has been organized to force sympathy strikes, I ask you "Who are the Conspirators?"

The twenty-six railroads centered at Chicago combined through their general managers with two great purposes in view : First, to reduce wages all over the country, and second, to put those who protested on the black list and forever bar the doors against them. This institution was formed prior to the organization of the A. R. U. Shortly after this institution was organized, reduction of wages began all over the country. I have here another report that I desire to read. Here is a copy of the original reduction made very shortly after this Manager's Association was perfected : Which acquainted the employees of a reduction of 15 to 33⅓ per cent in their wages, reducing the wages of section men and helpers in freight and roundhouses, etc., as low as 67½ cents per day.

I submit it is not possible for a man to provide for his wife, to rear his children as becomes an American citizen, on 67½ cents a day. He cannot live in a cottage (I know because I saw); he is compelled to live in a hovel such as a vagabond fox would not inhabit. He has got to subsist upon food that is not fit for a human being, and he is compelled to allow his children to grow up in ignorance because he does not get wages enough, notwithstanding he works hard and faithfully every day in the month, to buy clothes to make his children presentable, and his children, by the force of circumstances of which they are the victims, are compelled to grow up ignorant, and a great many of them drift into crime.

The foundations of this republic rest in the virtue and intelligence of the people. If multiplied thousands of working men are ground and crushed to an extent that they cannot educate their children, what a change a few generations will produce; and I want to say that the foundations of the republic will rest very insecurely then.

Let me call your attention to the fact that no two railroads reduce wages at the same time; they do not care to arouse too many employees at once and call public attention to the reduction. These reductions occurred every two weeks or so. They came up into the eastern part of the country and took in some of the railroads there, and then came to this part of the country. They took in the Chicago & Eastern Illinois road, then they took in the Northern Pacific (and, by the way, let me say that the Northern Pacific is the one corporation goose that has been plucked every time there has been a pinfeather in sight).

When some of these corporations have a courageous, manly body of men working for them, and they are afraid that a reduction will result in a strike, they avoid reducing the wages and go on and wreck the road. After they have wrecked the road they apply for a receiver, and then the court grants the receivership; then the court, on due application, orders a reduction of wages, and after the reduction has been ordered, there is another order issued restraining the men from quitting the employ of the company. Jenkins did not, however, issue an order restraining the company from discharging the men, and it's a mighty poor rule that won't work both ways.

No, that did not occur in Russia. That was here, under the stars and stripes. I addressed a meeting in the home of Judge Jenkins the other night at Milwaukee, and I said if justice were done him he would be wearing stripes and pounding rocks, and if that is contempt of court he is entitled to make the most of it. The other day he sat on the bench, and the court crier said, "God save this honorable court." I said "Amen. I do not know of any power this side of the Almighty that could save it."

That Northern Pacific reduction was a case of the court holding the men up while the corporation went through their pockets. But the reduction did not stop there. The Great Northern fell into line, but it did not last long there, because once in the history of labor the men had the sense to unify their forces. That was all that saved them. By the power of unified effort they succeeded in making a settlement that was perfectly amicable and perfectly satisfactory, so far as I know, to all concerned.

At the same time that there was a reduction on the Great Northern there was a reduction ordered on the Chicago & Great

Western, to take effect later. As soon as the men quit the Great Northern, this road decided that the atmosphere was not favorable for a reduction, and notwithstanding the fact that the reduction was ordered, it was not made, nor has it been made from that day to this.

Then a reduction was ordered on the Union Pacific, but they had a judge there who was an upright man, and his name commands my respect. I refer to Judge Caldwell. After exposing the rascality of the management, and showing that if the property was honestly managed, it could have paid its employees honest wages, he said, "There will be no reduction on this system if not another dollar is paid on the watered stock." There was no reduction, not because the corporation was not desirous of making it, but because between the corporation and the employees there was a judicial Gibraltar. If there were more judges of that character in the country, there would be more confidence in the courts.

So, when the delegates met, they were employed on roads some of which had already made a reduction, and others were going to make them, according to the carefully arranged program of the General Managers' Association, and when these delegates saw the horifying conditions at Pullman, they said, "We might as well strike and starve as work and starve; we would at least preserve our manhood."

The strike began on the 26th day of June. In just four days the Managers' Association was completely defeated. The American Railway Union was triumphant. There was, as the records show, not the slightest disorder or lawlessness up to that time. The Managers' Association saw they were defeated and something had to be done to rescue them from that dilemma, and something was done. The cars began to burn. I want to prove to you tonight that they were not burned by the members of the American Railway Union, nor by their sympathizers. There was no escape for the General Managers except by the torch of their emissaries, and I want to prove to you that it was done by their emissaries. The American Railway Union had everything to loose by arson, by riot, and by lawlessness, but the railway companies had everything to gain. They could then apply for an injunction. They could then arrest and imprison the leaders.

I made this statement in Chicago the other night in the presence of four thousand people, and a gentleman was in the audience who bore testimony to it. Captain Power, a high official in the fire department of the city of Chicago, came to me and said, "Debs, when the cars were burning and I was trying to put out the fire, I found a man trying to cut the hose, and I struck him and found that he was a deputy United States marshal, and was employed by the General Managers' Association."

We had eighty witnesses at Chicago, and among them high officials in the police and fire departments, to testify as to who lighted the fires and incited the riot and was responsible for the lawlessness.

There is an official report on file in the office of the mayor of Chicago, signed by two policemen who were deputized to clothe themselves in citizen's dress and find out who were setting fire to the box cars in Chicago, and at midnight they saw two men who had lighted a match and were about to set some cars afire, and they arrested them and found that they were both deputy United States marshals in the employ of the General Managers' Association. The gentlemen were there who testified to it under oath, but they did not get the chance to testify. While we could have continued the trial, and were anxious to continue the trial, and could have legally continued the trial, they refused to listen to any proposition under which the trial might have been continued.

The true conspirators will be known. Just now we are the conspirators, but there will be a shifting of the scenes, and the gentlemen who a little while ago waited in perfect composure for us to go to the penitentiary, may go there themselves before we get through with them.

The American Railway Union believes in the supremacy of the law. The American Railway Union is composed of manly American citizens. They believe in and are at all times ready to uphold our institution and if the old flag were assailed, if Old Glory was in peril, I do not hesitate to declare that no body of men would go to the front more quickly and more valiantly, than the men who make up the American Railway Union, and not only them, but the workingmen of the country generally, because they are the men who do the fighting, when there is any fighting to be done.

I wonder if Mr. Pullman could say as much for himself? I presume he would be a good deal like Mark Twain was at the time of the "late unpleasantness." He said, "I propose to suppress this rebellion if it costs every one of my wife's relatives." He would be patriotic by proxy. He would be a hero at very long range.

No, the A. R. U. is not responsible for the violence that was committed at Chicago. The A. R. U. did everything within its power to preserve order, to maintain the law, to prevent bloodshed; but on the 30th day of June, when all of the roads were paralyzed, (simply because the men in a body withdrew from the service of the Company) when that time came, and the General Managers realized that they were defeated and that the A. R. U. had compelled them to make some terms looking to a satisfactory adjustment of the existing trouble, they saw there was only one way in which defeat could be turned into victory; they had 4,200 deputy marshals sworn in, and the chief deputy marshal who swore them in, more than 2,000 of them, testified under oath that many of them were the toughest looking men he ever saw. They were dragged from the slums of the city of Chicago, clothed with United States authority, their pockets were filled with money and they were given a knowing look, and they went among the men who were congregated about, and then the trouble began.

They were the men who commenced all the trouble, and just as soon as the trouble began and the wires were burdened with the information that Chicago was in flames and under the rule of a mob, the law-abiding citizens said, "We must suppress that mob, and preserve rule and order." I am constrained to say that everything was peaceable, and the only evidence of riot was the presence of the militia, which had been called out.

We wanted no trouble. The Managers' Association wanted trouble; that was their only escape and they did not hesitate to employ the means that were required to relieve them, if they had to resort to bloodshed. "Truth crushed to earth will rise again." Let me ask you if the members of the A. R. U. had been led by a malicious motive, if they had been bent on destroying property, is it reasonable to suppose that they would have destroyed just one palace Pullman car. They were in the yard, they were just as easy of access, but there was not one of them destroyed. They were too expensive. The fire always originated in out of service hospital cars, which were not worth more than $25 apiece. They served the purpose of a conflagration and that was all that was required. They reasoned that Cook county would be legally responsible for every car destroyed. They would not lose anything by the conflagration but would be reimbursed in full. However, they have not yet brought their suit for damages and I apprehend that they are not going to bring any suit.

In the late trial there was sufficient to induce them to change their minds. When they bring these damage suits against the city of Chicago, they want to put on a fire escape equipment. The city of Chicago is loaded with evidence to show that they destroyed their own property, or at least that it was destroyed by plugs and thieves in their employ, and they are going to show that many of them are now in the service of the Company. They do not want any damages. There will be no suits brought; they have changed their minds very considerably the last few days. They did not know that they were going to be called on the witness stand, and they were a little the worst scared lot of managers I ever saw, and they were afflicted with a chronic lapse of memory. I know that a general managership is a position that is extremely exacting, but I did not know that it had such a demoralizing effect upon the mental faculties. Let me relate a little instance. We had five general managers on the stand. Three days before the strike occurred, the general managers met and the Pullman Association with them, and they formed an association. Mr. Wicks, the vice president of the Pullman Company, was there, and on account of the secret proceedings which took place, the meeting was called an emergency trial. This was on the 24th day of June.

Five of the General Managers were put on the stand and asked what Mr. Wicks, of the Pullman Company, was there for, and not one of them could remember. One of them did say that Mr. Wicks was there to tell them he had nothing to say. I know what he was there for, and so do you. He was there for the purpose of perfecting the partnership between the General Managers' Association and the Pullman Company. The General Managers' Association did not want the Pullman Company to settle. One word from the General Managers would have been sufficient to compel the Pullman Company to arbitrate its differences with its employees, but that word was not spoken.

I will tell you why the General Managers' Association went into partnership with the officials of the Pullman Company to starve their employees to death. I know whereof I speak. We had a detective or two of our own. The General Managers' Association had viewed with great alarm the rapid development of the A. R. U. They said, "This unification is going on all over the country. They have succeeded on the Great Northern. If this is permitted to go forward, it will not be long before they will have a voice in regulating wages," and that was just what the General Managers did not want to see. Their interest is in keeping the A. R. U. divided and quarrelling among themselves, and they have been very successful at it, I must say.

They understood the strength of the A. R. U. They thought they could snuff it out like a candle. When the trouble commenced the injunctions were issued. As a matter of course, it is a very easy matter to demoralize a well-disciplined system of working men. Take away their leaders and persuade them that all the well organized forces of society are against them and their defeat is accomplished. The A. R. U. had no friend. The A. R. U. stood by and for itself. I mean to say in that immediate vicinity. I know that here and there was a noble soul who had the courage to speak out and to invite abuse because of speaking out, but as a general proposition all the powers were against it.

It was a struggle that a body of working men were making for all humanity. They were fighting the battle that you will have to fight in a few years. Am I an alarmist? Let me read the words of another agitator. See what he says on the subject. You all know him, and you will not malign him, either. His name is Abraham Lincoln. You applaud him now, but they did not applaud him then. In 1864 the labor organizations made him an honorary member, and he wrote a letter in honor of this, and this is what he said:

I see in the near future a crisis approaching that unnerves me and causes me to tremble for the safety of my country. As a result of war, corporations have been enthroned and an era of corruption in high places will follow, and the money power of the country will endeavor to prolong its reign, working upon the prejudices of the people until all wealth is aggregated in a few hands and the republic is destroyed. I feel at this moment more anxiety for the safety of the country than ever before, even in the midst of war.

He saw with prophetic vision what the future had in store. When he wrote that letter he was denounced for it. He was maligned for being an agitator, but he spoke from the fullness of his patriotic heart, and if you do not believe that the prophecy has been entirely fulfilled, you will believe it before the lapse of many more years. The world is not just. It is a long way from being generous. I admit that we are making a little progress, but it is like a painted ship on a painted sea, impossible to tell whether we are moving at all; but I believe we are moving in the right direction.

To return to the subject: Injunctions were issued by the courts to restrain us from doing our duty, to demoralize our men, to defeat the cause of labor, and make the cause of corporations triumphant. What is an injunction? It is a law made by a judge. If you violate that injunction you are tried by that same judge, and in the federal court there is no appeal from that injunction. It does not matter whether the injunction is valid or not, you are compelled to obey it, and if you violate it you are arrested and sent to jail for contempt of court, so that every federal judge can be a czar.

You are not punished for committing a crime, but for contempt of court. I said when I was sentenced, "I am glad I am compelled to be guilty of contempt of such a contemptible court, or else I would have to be guilty of contempt of myself." I want to see the time come when our judicial tribunals will stand for justice.

When I was in jail at Chicago I had for a fellow prisoner a young boy 22 years of age. He had just been married a short time, lost his situation through no fault of his own, and he could not find work. His wife thought she could find something to do, but she did not have clothes enough to make herself presentable. In leaving his cottage and going toward the city, he often passed a second hand store, and he saw an old second hand coat swinging in the breeze, that was used for a sign. He passed it and thought of his wife, and one day, when he thought no one saw him, he stole it, but as a matter of course he was arrested and given twelve months in jail.

A short time ago there was a shortage of two millions of dollars in the Santa Fe railroad. Mr. Rhinehart was president; he was the responsible official. He did not plead "Not guilty." He was permitted to resign. He lives in Boston. He basks in the smiles of the aristocrats there. He is a social lion. Everybody doffs his hat in his presence. He is a colossal scoundrel. He ought to have gone to the penitentiary for twenty years, but he was not even arrested. He was not enjoined. He was not punished for contempt of court. He is a rich man. The poor man who stole the coat was friendless. We have a law for the rich and another law for the poor. If I had about two hours' time I would demonstrate it to you.

The poor man who stole a coat because his wife was suffering went to jail for twelve months. He did not have the money with which to buy justice. In many of the courts of our country justice is for sale to the highest bidder. I have a faculty for giving the promptings of my heart, and some people like me for it and some don't, but it does not matter to me. That boy stole a coat, and in doing so he only responded to the promptings of his heart; he simply was obedient to the dictates of his feelings. I want to say that if I had been in his place and had tramped all the streets in search of work and my wife wanted a coat and I could not get it for her honestly, I would steal it, and it seems to me that if a perfectly honest judge dispenses justice, Rhinehart, the president of the Santa Fe railroad, would be in the penitentiary and the boy who stole the coat would be promoted.

Do you notice that there are no injunctions issued against corporations? Injunctions are exceedingly convenient instrumentalities to be employed when workingmen resist reduction and degradation. We have a law on the statute books called the anti-trust law. Senator Sherman said that this law was never intended to be used against the workingmen. Do you know of any trust that has been suppressed by it? They have grown more rapidly since that was made a law than before. When the great strike was organized last summer, it was discovered that that was the very law to be used against the workingmen, and they used that law with which to crush the workingmen.

So far as its effect upon trusts is concerned, it is not perceptible, I think, not visible to the eye. When working men strike to resist injustice, then it is found that they have combined in restraint of trade and are punishable by fine and imprisonment, or death; but the injunction serves another purpose. This has become a government by injunctions. I said at the time I was arrested, "If I and my colleagues had violated any law, let us be tried by a jury of our peers, and if we are guilty we will go to the penitentiary." They knew that there was no jury that would convict us, but they had to put us into jail. How did they do it? They issued an injunction. If you have never read it you ought to get a copy of it. I could not have avoided violating that injunction unless I would have died right suddenly after it was served on me. Only a corpse would have escaped conviction of contempt of court for the violation of that injunction. I know there are a great many people who wish I were one.

That injunction restrained me from writing a letter, sending a telegram, holding a conversation with any of the employees of any of the railroads. I think it even intended to restrain me from holding communion with myself. I was persuaded, for a time at least while I was thinking about the matter, that I had better not be indiscreet enough to think aloud lest some one should hear me and report me, and I should be guily of contempt of court.

I called on two of the leading lawyers of the city, and they said,

"Proceed as you have been doing; you have been leading a perfectly
lawful life." I took their advice and got six months for it, but I am
not sorry for it. I have nothing to regret. I said at the time "If it
is six months or six years, or the rest of my natural life, it will not
cause me to flinch a bit."

This injuncion struck down every citizen's right, and I could
not help being in contempt of that order without being in supreme
contempt of myself. I said, as between the court and myself, "I will
stand by Debs and take the consequences." Then they sent men
down to my home at Terra Haute, Indiana, where I was born and
reared and lived all the days of my life, to find out what they could
ascertain in regard to my character that would be useful in evidence.

Terra Haute is a city of 38,000 population, and after they had
scoured that place, called on all the ministers and lawyers and the
city officials, they came back and said they could not find a soul to
testify against my character. I do not believe there is a man, woman
or child in Terra Haute but will testify to my being an honest man.
These statements would not be in good taste but for the fact that the
capitalistic press of this country has deluged me with misrepresentation and slander. They sought to destroy utterly my influence, and
they sought to do it by having the people of this country believe that
I was a monster of depravity.

I could have their favors if I desired them. I could have the
opinion of being a gentleman, instead of an agitator and a revolu-
tionist. I could bask in the smiles of the General Managers of this
country, but I do not desire or expect their favors. My duty lies in
another direction. They are merely employees themselves. They are
obedient, and compelled to be obedient, to the money power above
them. They do as they are compelled to do. They have no right
to have a heart. They have got to be men who are made of cast-
iron, and if any one of them shows any tendency of having a heart
and humanity within, they remove him and put an iron man in his
place, who does as he is ordered to do. In our days, if a man becomes the general manager of one of these railroad corporations, he
has got to extinguish the last spark of humanity that glows or burns
within his breast.

The time will come in the very near future when many of the
people who have taken their position against us will find out that
they themselves are in danger; they will find that they are con-
fronted by the very power that has for the time being crushed us.

There is a centralization going forward in this country that is a
menace to the republic, by processes that will not bear investigation.
The wealth of this country is centralizing in a very few hands. The
process is exceedingly rapid. In proportion as this century
goes forward, pauperism increases throughout the land. In the history of no country is there a record of such an accumulation of

wealth as that which has taken place in this country in the past fifty years.

The multi-millionaires are multiplying and so are the mendicants. The palace and the hovel go up side by side. No trouble about the resources of this country. No trouble about wealth. There is no excuse for the conditions that now prevail. They are traceable in direct line to the powers that are gained over the people, and unless something is done to resist their operations, the republic will be destroyed.

I am not an alarmist, but I believe it is time to offer a cry of warning. The cry will go up "He is a demagogue." I accept the compliment. From that standpoint I am a demagogue and expect to be. For the past ten years, when a man has had the courage to protest against wrong in high places, the cry of "Anarchy" goes up, but that loses its force. The people are beginning to see the gravity of the situation that confronts them. There has got to be a change and a very radical change.

In these small western places you may not appreciate the necessity for it, but go to the centers of population, to Chicago, New York or San Francisco, and see what wretchedness, what squalor, what poverty and degradation prevail there. It is increasing day by day in exact ratio as the wealth of the country centralizes in a few hands. Rapidly we are approaching that period in our history where we will have but the two classes, the rich and the extremely poor. The working people of this country are getting poorer and the rich richer and what we call the middle classes of this country are going to disappear entirely.

Labor saving machinery was designed to be a blessing to the world, but on account of the greed of the corporations, it is getting to be a curse. We no longer have the shoemakers and the village blacksmiths and the small stores in the large cities. They have all disappeared. You have the great stores and the great enterprises, everything running to trusts. You simply have the trust and the employees. A man has got to have an immense capital to start in business. Immense capital is required to carry forward the industrial enterprises of the times, all of which has the tendency to enslave the people of the country. I believe the time has come when we should see the situation precisely as it is. It does no good to try and deceive ourselves. Sooner or later the haggard truth will confront us. Better prepare for what I conceive to be the inevitable.

As a matter of course, I cannot lose faith in the destiny of the republic. I am so constituted that the more the obstacles multiply, the greater my will and determination. I cannot become despondent nor can I surrender. I know there are thousands of men when the time comes who will be equal to every duty that the hour may impose upon them, with perfect faith that everything will come right in the end, and that the very influences that are in operation that now seem dangerous will be found favorable to the cause of emancipation.

It was said in the days of the Coliseum by the Romans that "When falls the Coliseum, Rome will fall, and when Rome falls, falls the world." I prefer to say that when the American home falls, falls the republic, and when the republic falls, the greatest and brightest light that ever passed through the pathway of progress goes out forever.

Ruskin says the nation lives in the cottage. That used to be true, but it is no longer true. There is a large proportion of the nation that lives in hovels, holes and dens. It ought to live in a cottage.

I believe that the most beautiful and elevating influences of the world are in the home. I love to cultivate the cottage, the hearth and the fireside. It must be admitted that workingmen have not always been true to themselves. They have not taken advantage of the opportunities given them. Every workingman ought to have a library in these days of cheap literature; ought to expand his mental horizon, and improve his mind. , I know of railroad men who would rather sit around the roundhouse and tell about "runs" that never have been made nor ever will be. I have said that no man ever went to the penitentiary in this world who spent his leisure hours at his fireside. This is the one source of enjoyment that I possess. I have one of the loveliest homes in the world. My father and my mother and my wife and my sisters and my brother are all there, and no matter how trying the ordeal may be, that is the one place where I can go where I am always welcome.

Every workingman, no matter how humble his home may be, can make it blossom with affection. I can see no more touching picture than the workingman returning to his home and seeing the light at long range, and as he enters the door feeling the hearty welcome that is accorded him ; to see him draw up his chair to the fireside and read to his wife, and cultivate the graces of home, and wake up strengthened and refreshed in the morning.

I wish the workingmen of the country would pay more attention to the homes. Be true to the home and the home will be true to you. Spend your leisure time there. Take up a book and make up your mind to study it and learn something more than that that is required to perform your work and furnish you with the necessaries of life. Try it for twelve months and you will thank me for the suggestion. I know whereof I speak.

Workingmen must hew out their own way to emancipation. If the workingmen would be free, they themselves must strike the blow, and every man must free himself. You cannot be freed by proxy. Every man has got to solve the labor problem and solve it for himself. There is no darkness but ignorance. A workingman who is ignorant and dependent is in slavery. The very instant that he begins to take advantage of his surroundings, that very instant he begins to solve the labor problem and hew out his way to emancipation.

Those who think must govern those who toil. I want the working men of this country to mix some thought with their toil. I want them to follow the light of their own judgment. I for my part had rather depend upon my own judgment and go wrong than to go right following some one else. We do not need labor leaders. Let every man cultivate self-reliance; depend upon himself. If we do that right along, we will have a race of sturdy men who will be freemen.

If we would be really free, we should strike the shackles of bondage from the women of our country. We are not unmindful of women. We decorate them with rare jewels, but we keep them in political serfdom. Let us decorate them with that rare gem, political equality. If they do not choose to exercise this power, it is for them to decide. That time is coming in the very near future, and you will not be willing to admit that you opposed it. If a woman has not got a right to vote, where did we get ours? And if women have not got a right to vote, we are not quite civilized. We are making a little progress. I believe all the signs of the times are sure, and I believe that after a while the world will be fit to live in.

We have too much cupidity and selfishness. Men ought to have noble aspirations. This struggle, this continual conflict, each for himself, each willing to trample over the prostrate body of his fellows just to supply the material necessities of life, is continually going on. I want to see conditions under which we will do more to cultivate the intellect, the heart, the soul, the family relation, the home; when we will be less greedy, less selfish, nearer just than we are now.

I believe some progress is being made in that direction. I believe the day is coming when the workingman shall stand as free and independent as any in the land, and when he shall be rewarded for his toil of brain and hand.

A labor day is coming, when a workingman shall stand,
  As free and independent as any in the land;
When he shall be rewarded for his toil of brain and hand,
  For the Right is marching on.

A labor day is coming, don't you hear the grand refrain,
  Rounding through the country from the Golden Gate to Maine.
That workingmen are free, having broken every chain?
  For the Truth is marching on.

A labor day is coming, when Truth shall hold full sway,
  When Justice full enthroned, like the noontide god of day,
Shall set no more forever, for its coming let us pray,
  For the Right is marching on.

A labor day is coming, when our starry flag shall wave,
  Above a land where famine no longer digs a grave;
Where money is not master, nor a workingman a slave,
  For the Truth is marching on.

There are those who seek to discourage. There are those who seek to dishearten the men who are trying to reform the world. There are those who have no sympathy with the movement that is designed to make conditions better. To use a phrase: "They are not in it." This makes me think of a line that I saw the other day about one of those selfish men who was not in it:

"They built a church at his very door.
  He wasn't in it.
They got up a scheme to help the poor.
  He wasn't in it.
He said if they wasted each golden minute,
  He wasn't in it.

A hearse drove up the street one day,
  And he was in it.
The funeral trappings were grand and gay,
  And he was in it.
St. Peter met him on the way,
He said, "Your ticket reads to—well,
 · The elevator goes down in a minute."
  And he was in it.

My friends, I hope some of the words I have uttered have found their way to your hearts. I know there are those of you who disagree with me, yet I am one of those who believe that men and women can differ honestly and yet grasp each other's hand in genuine friendship.

In all the forests there are no two leaves that are just alike, nor two grains of sand on all the seashore that are just alike, and among all these myriads of minds there are no two working alike. We can disagree, and yet we can respect each other. Speak the truth. Speak the facts. I know that you will draw your own inferences, and when the final verdict is rendered, I have no doubt it will be on the side of right and justice.

I believe I know what my duty is, and in my humble way I am going to try and fulfill it. I have sympathy for the struggling men and women of the country and I am going to do what little lies in my power to ameliorate their condition. Every man who is in the right, whether he is black or white, if he is doing his level best, is my brother, and I am going to do what little I can to improve his condition and to contribute to his happiness.

With you, I hope that the dawn of a better day is near at hand, and I have faith that the night of slavery is on the wane, and the dawn of the day of emancipation is near.

Permit me to thank you, not with my lips merely, but from the depths of a grateful heart, for the patience and the kindness with which you have listened to me, and whether you agree with me or not, I bid you one and all good night, God-speed.

www.ingramcontent.com/pod-product-compliance
Lightning Source LLC
Chambersburg PA
CBHW031157090426
42738CB00008B/1371